SURFER
OF THE
CENTURY

THE LIFE OF DUKE KAHANAMOKU

BY ELLIE CROWE

ILLUSTRATIONS BY RICHARD WALDREP

Lee & Low Books Inc. • New York

ACKNOWLEDGMENTS

For information on surfing and the thrill of riding mountainous waves, I would like to thank surfers and big wave surfing champions George Downing, Ray Rasmussen, Eric Bennet, and Tony and Tammy Moniz from the Faith Riding Surf School, Waikīkī, Hawai'i. I would also like to thank Earl Maikahikinapāmaikalā Tenn, liaison for the estate of Nadine Kahanamoku, and Sandra Kimberley Hall, who shared their knowledge of Duke with me. Many thanks to Louise May, Editor in Chief at Lee & Low Books, for her enthusiasm, painstaking research, and excellent input. And a special thank you to my husband, Will, for all his help with ideas and editing, always. —E.C.

Thank you to Ben Finney, Professor Emeritus of Anthropology, University of Hawai'i at Mānoa, for his assistance in the preparation of this book, and to Donald Love and Mālama Pono Ltd., for permission to use images of Duke Kahanamoku.

AUTHOR'S SOURCES

Brennan, Joseph L. *Duke: The Life Story of Duke Kahanamoku*. Honolulu: Ku Pa'a Publishing, 1994.
———. *Duke Kahanamoku: Hawai'i's Golden Man*. Honolulu: Hogarth Press, 1974.
Finney, Ben, and James D. Houston. *Surfing: A History of the Ancient Hawaiian Sport*. Rohnert Park, CA: Pomegranate
     Artbooks, 1996.
Hall, Sandra Kimberley. *Duke: A Great Hawaiian*, Honolulu: Bess Press, 2004.
———, and Greg Ambrose. *Memories of Duke: The Legend Comes to Life*. Honolulu: Bess Press, 1995.
Kahanamoku, Duke Paoa, and Joe Brennan. *Duke Kahanamoku's World of Surfing*. New York: Grosset & Dunlop, 1968.
Timmons, Grady. *Waikiki Beachboy*. Honolulu: Editions Limited, 1989.
Young, Nat. *The History of Surfing*. Angourie, Australia: Palm Beach Press, 1983.

QUOTATION SOURCES

Several quotations in the book are from interviews with Duke Kahanamoku conducted by Joseph L. Brennan, Kahanamoku's longtime friend and biographer.

p. 11: "I'd like . . . got it." Quoted in Brennan, *Duke: The Life Story of Duke Kahanamoku*, p. 22.

p. 18: "What are . . . clocks?" Ibid., p. 33.
     "Coming down!" Kahanamoku family Web site: http://www.hawaiianswimboat.com.

p. 22: "Hello, . . . joining us." Quoted in Brennan, *Duke: The Life Story of Duke Kahanamoku*, p. 40.
     "Waiter, please . . . Kahanamoku." Ibid.

p. 27: "Jimmy . . . care of." Duke Kahanamoku interview, 1965. Reported in *Honolulu Star-Bulletin*, August 23, 1965.

p. 28: "Kahanamoku wanted . . . starting platform." Quoted in Brennan, *Duke: The Life Story of Duke Kahanamoku*, p. 52.
     "Where've you . . . been sleeping." Ibid.

p. 33: "Man overboard!" Brennan, *Duke: The Life Story of Duke Kahanamoku*, p. 71.

p. 34: "unusually . . . extremities," Quoted in Brennan, *Duke: The Life Story of Duke Kahanamoku*, p. 87.

p. 39: "for the . . . sport." Athletes' Olympic Oath. International Olympic Committee Web site:
     http://www.olympic.org/uk/utilities/faq_detail_uk.asp?rdo_cat=10_39_0.

p. 42: "the most . . . the world." Newport Beach, California, Chief of Police J. A. Porter, June 15, 1925. Quoted in Brennan,
     Duke: The Life Story of Duke Kahanamoku, p. 156.

p. 46: "No matter . . . spread aloha." Rabbit Kekai. *Surfer* magazine, vol. 40, no. 10, October 1999.
     Duke's Creed of Aloha. Message printed on back of Kahanamoku's business cards.

LEE & LOW BOOKS Inc., 95 Madison Avenue, New York, NY 10016, leeandlow.com
Manufactured in China by O.G. Printing Production Limited, March 2013
Book design by David and Susan Neuhaus/NeuStudio. Book production by The Kids at Our House.
The text is set in 13-point Venis. The illustrations are rendered in gouache with colored pencil detailing.
(HC) 10 9 8 7 6 5 4 3   (PB) 10 9 8 7 6 5 4 3 2 1   First Edition
Library of Congress Cataloging-in-Publication Data
Crowe, Ellie.
Surfer of the century : the life of Duke Kahanamoku / by Ellie Crowe ; illustrations by Richard Waldrep. — 1st ed.
p. cm.
Summary: "A biography of Hawaiian Duke Kahanamoku, five-time Olympic swimming champion from the early 1900s who is also considered worldwide as the 'father of modern surfing'"—Provided by publisher.
ISBN 978-1-58430-276-6 (hardcover)   ISBN 978-1-60060-461-4 (paperback)
1. Kahanamoku, Duke, 1890–1968. 2. Swimmers—Hawaii—Biography. 3. Surfers—Hawaii—Biography. I. Waldrep, Richard, ill. II. Title.
GV838.K35C76 2007
797.3'2092—dc22   [B]   2006036562

To Micah, Luke, and Sydney, who love riding the blue waves of Hawai'i —E.C.

To my daughter, Madeline, Maddy, "Maddo" —R.W.

Surfing—body, board or otherwise—is a sport that is in a class by itself. And for those who indulge in it, here is a wish that the surf may always be breaking big, fast, clean and fine for you.   —Duke Kahanamoku

Surf's up!

Eager surfers gripped their wooden surfboards and stared out at the monster waves. Spawned far out at sea, the thirty-foot "Bluebirds" streaked across miles of ocean in a solid line, crashing in white foam on Waikīkī Beach. Such huge waves occurred only on extraordinary occasions, the result of underwater earthquakes or volcanic eruptions. Who dared surf the Bluebirds?

Only one surfer mastered the gigantic waves that day in 1917—Duke Kahanamoku. He rode a thundering Bluebird for almost two miles, from the deep blue ocean to the white sand beach.

The Pacific Ocean was Duke's backyard. Born in 1890 in Honolulu, on the Hawaiian island of O'ahu, Duke Paoa Kahanamoku lived with his family across the road from Waikīkī Beach. Duke's childhood was filled with *aloha*. His parents were loving and supportive. He had five brothers, three sisters, and more than thirty cousins with whom to play. Neighbors helped one another and got together often, sharing the bananas, coconuts, taro, and sweet potatoes they grew in their gardens and the fish, crabs, squid, and octopuses they caught in the ocean.

When he was four years old, Duke learned to swim in the old Hawaiian way. His father and uncle took him in an outrigger canoe, tied a rope around his waist, and tossed him into the ocean. Wiggling like a little tadpole, Duke made his way back to the canoe.

Duke's mother told him never to be afraid of the water and to go out as far as he wanted. His father said the mighty shark was their family's Hawaiian guardian and would protect him. Swimming each day, Duke soon learned to surf, dive, and hold his breath underwater for minutes at a time.

aloha: *love, kindness, grace, affection, compassion; also a traditional Hawaiian greeting and farewell*

In school Duke struggled with his lessons, but in the ocean he was a star. As soon as the school bell rang, he raced to the beach and dived into the blue waves. The ocean was a second home to Duke, and he was happiest when he was swimming.

By the time he was a teenager, Duke was a very fast swimmer. His tall, strong body was designed for swimming. His large hands scooped through the water, while his big feet, like fins, propelled him along.

Duke had a natural talent, and he was determined to use it. He wanted to win races. He wanted to be a champion swimmer. Many of his friends could swim fast. The difference between swimming fast and winning races would be dedication and hard work.

Duke pushed himself to get better, swimming miles through the ocean day after day until his arm and leg muscles burned. He dropped out of high school and started working on the beach, making and selling surfboards. He earned enough money to help pay his family's bills, and he had plenty of time to swim. Soon Duke swam faster than all his friends, and he longed for an opportunity to race the best swimmers from the mainland United States.

When several top Australian swimmers visited Hawai'i in 1910, Duke studied their special crawl stroke. Deciding that their stiff-legged kick used up too much energy, Duke developed the flutter kick, a flexible-knee version of the Australian crawl. He called his new swimming style the Hawaiian crawl and joked that his kick was the Kahanamoku kick.

One afternoon in the summer of 1911, Bill Rawlins, a Honolulu attorney with an interest in swimming, was watching Duke slash through the ocean. He couldn't believe how fast the young man swam. Fetching a stopwatch, he asked Duke and two of his friends to swim a measured 100-yard course. When Rawlins timed the swimmers, he was stunned. Duke had shown amazing speed. Rawlins thought Duke had the makings of a swimming champion.

"I'd like to coach you," Rawlins told Duke.

Duke's heart leaped. "It's a deal if you think I've got it," he said.

They closed the agreement with a handshake and a smile.

Duke and his two friends joined with other eager swimmers to form a swim team. Rawlins told the group that to get recognition for any records they set, they had to belong to a surf club. Duke had tried earlier to join the Healani Club and had been refused membership even though he knew some of the members. To the club he was just a penniless beachboy. Duke was hurt but managed to shrug off the rejection.

Acting on Rawlins's advice, the members of the swimming team organized the Hui Nalu, Club of the Waves. They called it the "poor man's surf club" because they had no clubhouse and met under a *hau* tree at Waikīkī Beach.

Sitting in the shade of the tree, Duke and his friends worked on building bigger surfboards with sleeker lines and better balance. Duke developed a huge, 16-foot, 114-pound board that handled well. In Waikīkī's rolling waves, the beachboys worked on new surfing maneuvers: standing on a board backward, stepping from board to board, sliding left and right with the waves, doing headstands, and riding tandem with another person, usually a pretty girl, on the surfer's shoulders.

In 1910 Hawai'i's sports clubs had voted to form the Hawaiian Amateur Athletic Union. The creation of the AAU-Hawai'i made Hawaiian athletes eligible for national Amateur Athletic Union events and possible participation in the Olympics.

The AAU-Hawai'i decided to hold its first contest, a swim meet, on August 12, 1911. This was Duke's big chance. He would compete against nationally ranked swimmers from the mainland United States.

The race meant a lot to Hawai'i. There were many gifted watermen on the islands, but no Hawaiian had ever been recognized by the world as a top swimming champion. Rawlins was confident Duke could beat the swimmers from the mainland and make it onto the U.S. team for the 1912 Olympic Games in Stockholm, Sweden.

On the day of the swim meet, excited spectators gathered at Honolulu's wharves. Hawai'i did not have an Olympic-sized swimming pool, so the contest was held in the ocean, with the swimmers racing between two piers in the harbor. The crowd hummed with eager anticipation as the start of the 100-yard freestyle race grew near.

Heart thudding, Duke stood at the edge of the wharf.

BAM! The pistol shot rang out.

Duke's family and friends screamed his name as the swimmers hit the water. They were neck to neck until Duke, fierce with determination, forged ahead. He plowed through the water like a speedboat, a mound of water rising in front of his chest, a white wake of foam trailing behind him. Duke shot to the finish line with lightning speed.

Pulling himself out of the water, Duke was puzzled by the judges' startled expressions. Then they shouted that Duke had broken the world record! He had swum the race in 55.4 seconds, shaving 4.6 seconds off the official time. Duke grinned, shaking his head in amazement. The cheering spectators hugged him and clapped his back. Everyone wanted to touch him, be a part of his success.

 By the end of the day Duke had shattered three long-standing AAU freestyle swimming records: the 100-yard, the 50-yard, and the 220-yard. The judges declared that his times were fast enough to qualify for the Olympic tryouts.

Duke was bursting with excitement. How great it would be to compete in the Olympics and bring home the gold for Hawai'i!

For weeks reporters followed Duke around the beach at Waikīkī, taking his photo and trying to interview him. The reporters found it difficult to get Duke to say much. He was too shy and humble to talk about himself.

Then bad news arrived. Duke's new records were so amazing, Amateur Athletic Union officials in New York refused to believe his times. "What are you using for stopwatches?" a sarcastic official asked. "Alarm clocks?"

Duke was shattered. He feared everything was over. Trying to drown his disappointment, Duke grabbed his surfboard and headed to the ocean. "Coming down!" he yelled as he launched his board over the crests of the waves. His friends made way for him. They knew how he felt.

Meanwhile word of Duke's record-breaking swimming times had swept the athletic world. AAU officials, curious about the young, untrained swimmer, wanted to see Duke swim for themselves. They invited him to the mainland to try out for the United States Olympic team.

Thrilled by the news, Duke and his family huddled around the kitchen table. Money was tight. They didn't know how they would pay for Duke's boat trip to California. Soon friends and supporters gathered to help. Coach Rawlins arranged benefit potluck dinners and made generous donations. Duke's friends raised cash by performing a play on the deck of an abandoned ship. Along with contributions from others, enough money was raised to send Duke to the mainland.

Filled with Olympic dreams, Duke said good-bye to family and friends and boarded an ocean steamer to California in early February 1912. Rawlins's work as an attorney kept him from traveling, so Duke was accompanied by two members of his swim team. Lew Henderson acted as manager and Dude Miller was the swimming trainer.

In Los Angeles, Duke stared wide-eyed at the crowded streets. This big city was very different from his island home. Reporters described Duke as a strange-looking, dark-skinned native from distant lands. People stared at him. Restaurant waiters pretended not to see him. After a few awkward meals, Duke decided to eat alone in his hotel room so that Henderson and Miller would not be embarrassed by his presence.

Duke's first qualifying race was in Chicago. When he got off the train from Los Angeles, the icy winter wind bit through his thin suit coat. Looking for a way to stay warm, Duke stuffed cardboard under his coat and kept it tightly buttoned. The cardboard was secret until Duke unthinkingly pulled off his coat in the changing room of the Chicago swim stadium. Everyone laughed as the cardboard fell to the floor.

Duke burned with embarrassment but told himself to focus on the swimming. He knew he was as good as any swimmer alive. Duke won the 100-yard freestyle race in 57 seconds. He was on his way to being accepted for the Olympic team.

Pittsburgh was even colder than Chicago. Upon arriving, Duke hurried into a restaurant to order a bowl of hot soup. The waiter took one look at Duke's dark skin and asked him to leave. Humiliated, he headed for the door.

Just then someone called, "Hello, Duke! How about joining us?" Duke turned to see a friend who visited Hawai'i every few years. People were staring, but his friend said, "Waiter, please have another place set at my table for the sensational Hawaiian swimmer, Duke Kahanamoku." Duke downed his food as fast as he could. He thanked his friend and his friend's companions, invited them to visit him in Hawai'i, and hurriedly left the restaurant.

That night in the Pittsburgh stadium Duke was tense with anticipation. He was competing against world-class swimmers, and every one of them wanted a place on the Olympic team. Duke dived into the pool, ready to prove himself. The water was freezing. His left leg cramped, and to his horror Duke found he couldn't swim. He came to a crippled halt and had to be pulled from the pool. Surrounded by the booing crowd, Duke looked down sadly at his big, cold feet. He had always thought he could depend on his body, but this time it had failed him.

The next day Duke decided to swim around the pool before his first race to get his body used to the icy temperature. The crowd jeered, calling him a show-off. Duke tried to ignore the taunts. He climbed out of the pool and stood alone, waiting for the other swimmers to line up. His mind went back home. He thought of all the people who had paid for his trip, and his family, friends, and coach, who were praying for him to succeed. He couldn't disappoint them.

From the moment Duke hit the water, he swam with spectacular speed. Used to open-ocean racing, he lost time on turns, but made up the loss with his furious arm strokes and powerful flutter kicks. He won the 100-yard race and then the 50-yard race, beating the world records with seconds to spare. Now on his side, the spectators screamed their support.

The endless swimming and hard work had paid off. Duke was going to the Olympic Games in Stockholm! He would be the first Hawaiian ever to swim in the Olympics, competing against the strongest swimmers from around the world. The competition would be fierce, but Duke ached to test himself against these legendary athletes.

The Olympic ship, the SS *Finland,* arrived in Sweden in July 1912. The sky was overcast and the water looked dark and cold. Crowds of reporters rushed the athletes as they milled around on the ship's deck. The reporters had many names for Duke—human fish, half-man-half-fish, merman, paddlewheel steamer— and they showered him with questions about his amazing speed. Duke answered the reporters' questions as best he could.

Escaping to the top deck, Duke found a sheltered spot and sat talking with a new friend, Native American track-and-field star Jim Thorpe. Like Duke, Jim was a natural athlete, virtually self-trained. They had both made it onto the Olympic team at a time when people of color rarely competed for the United States.

"Jimmy," Duke said, "you can run, jump, throw things, and carry the ball. You do everything. So why don't you swim too?"

"Duke, I saved that for you to take care of," Jim said, grinning.

Summers in Sweden have almost twenty-four hours of daylight, and Duke found it hard to get enough sleep at night. So on the morning of his first race, he decided to take a nap in his cabin.

Crowds had gathered at the Stockholm Olympic swimming venue. The Swedish royal family, diplomats, military officers, and thousands of fans were there to watch the popular 100-meter freestyle race.

"Kahanamoku wanted on the starting platform," an official announced over the public address system. After a few moments the official repeated loudly, "Kahanamoku wanted on the starting platform."

Duke did not appear. Frantically his teammates searched the swimming stadium. Then they raced to the ship and searched there. Michael McDermott, the U.S. breaststroke champion, found Duke and shook him awake.

At the stadium, Duke pushed through the crowds and approached the starting official.

"Where've you been?" the frowning official demanded.

"I'm—I'm sorry," Duke apologized. "I've been sleeping."

The official told him he was too late.

Silence fell on the crowd. Duke thought he would die. Everything he had worked so hard for—gone in an instant. He had missed his race in the Olympics!

Suddenly Cecil Healy, Australia's star swimmer, called out for Duke to be allowed in the race. Healy refused to swim unless Duke competed, even though Duke was his main threat.

It seemed as though no one in the stadium breathed. Duke stared at the ground and waited for a minute that seemed to go on forever.

Finally the official relented, giving Duke a curt nod.

Adrenaline pumping through his body, Duke lined up with Bretting and Ramme from Germany, Longworth and Healy from Australia, and Huszagh from the United States. The starting pistol cracked, and the six swimmers hit the water. Duke was up first from his dive, slicing through the water. At twenty-five meters, Duke was well ahead. Then from the corner of his eye he saw Healy coming up fast. Duke powered on, ripping across the pool, his body lifting up and forward. The crowd roared. With Healy on his heels, Duke slammed the finish line, clocking 63.4 seconds, a new Olympic record. Healy was 1.2 seconds behind. Duke had won Olympic gold!

King Gustav of Sweden was so impressed with Duke that he personally awarded him the gold medal and placed the wreath of victory on his head. Duke smiled and stammered his thanks. His smile grew wider when the king also honored Duke's friend Jim Thorpe, who had won two gold medals.

Suddenly Duke was an international champion, and sports fans everywhere wanted to see the big Hawaiian swim. Duke obliged, competing in swimming pools all over Europe and even in the Seine River in Paris. Back in the United States, he taught swimmers on the East Coast to surf. Although public beaches and pools on the mainland were mostly closed to people of color, Duke's exhibitions were a first step toward integrating these facilities.

To the world Duke became a symbol of Hawai'i. When newspapers reported that Duke was a descendant of ancient Polynesian kings, he modestly replied that he was just a beachboy from Waikīkī. Duke also tried hard to present a good image and live up to people's expectations. He slipped up only once. Traveling on a slow-moving steamer, Duke found the sparkling ocean just too tempting. When the boat's engine stalled and was being repaired, he dived over the side for a quick swim. The rough sea quickly pulled Duke and the ship in opposite directions. Duke swam as hard as he could, but he couldn't make it back. With passengers yelling, "Man overboard!" he was rescued by a lifeboat.

Duke's return to Honolulu in October 1912 was triumphant. Thousands of supporters met the ship. Cannons boomed. Music filled the air. Duke's family and friends rushed the gangway and piled colorful leis around his neck. The sweet-smelling flowers reached right up to Duke's eyes. He had to peek over them to see the welcoming crowd.

Duke received offers to turn professional and be paid for competing in swimming meets. But the Olympic Games were open only to unpaid amateurs, so Duke refused. He wanted to compete in the 1916 Olympics in Berlin, Germany.

While he trained Duke needed to earn a living. He didn't have many work skills. He had left school early, and the ocean was all he knew. Finally Duke found a job assisting surveyors in the Honolulu Water Department. Each day after work he ran to Waikīkī Beach to swim.

In late 1914 the Australian swim team was training feverishly for the Berlin Olympics. They invited Duke to Australia to compete in swim meets with them. They also wanted him to demonstrate his Hawaiian crawl and flutter kick. Duke accepted eagerly.

Arriving in Sydney, Duke was surprised by the enthusiastic reception he received from the Australians. He promised to do his best to please everybody. During his thirty-three race tour, the sports stadiums of Sydney, Melbourne, and Brisbane were packed with appreciative crowds. Duke gave outstanding performances in race after race and laughed when he read news reports about his "unusually large pedal extremities," which gave power to his Kahanamoku kick. Duke's sportsmanship and good nature won him many new fans.

The Australians had been so welcoming and generous, Duke wanted to do something to repay them. Although some Australians knew about surfing before his visit, Duke noticed that they were not taking advantage of their wonderful, big surf. He thought this was very unusual. Hawaiians had been riding the waves for at least a thousand years. Duke decided he would introduce the Australians to board surfing, the sport of the ancient Hawaiian kings.

No surfboard was available, so Duke bought a sugar pine plank and spent a day shaping an 8-foot, 9-inch board. Word spread that the Hawaiian swimming champion was going to ride ocean waves on a board, and crowds of curious people gathered at Freshwater Beach in Sydney. The amazed spectators cheered with delight as Duke rode the board down the long, steep face of a wave and across the cove, continually beating the break.

By the end of the day Duke had soared, glided, drifted, and stood on his head, all while riding his surfboard. For a finale he invited a girl to sit on his shoulder, and they rode a wave to shore while the onlookers clapped and shouted loudly.

Back in Hawai'i Duke continued to train for the Olympics. When he wasn't swimming or working, Duke and his Hui Nalu friends could be found at Waikīkī Beach, teaching visitors to surf. Surfing was catching on as a sport on the east and west coasts of the United States, and Duke loved sharing the excitement of riding the waves.

Duke's dream of competing in the 1916 Berlin Olympics came to an end when the games were canceled due to World War I, which had been raging in Europe since 1914. When the United States entered the war in 1917, Duke traveled throughout the mainland as a Red Cross volunteer in water safety and lifesaving techniques. He also competed with other swimmers to raise money for the Red Cross and to purchase U.S. war bonds.

Duke was twenty-eight when the war ended in 1918, and some feared he was too old to compete in the 1920 Olympic Games in Antwerp, Belgium. But Duke wasn't ready to give up. He trained and swam himself into top condition. Once again Duke won Olympic gold for the United States, speeding through the water far ahead of his competitors and clocking 60.4 seconds for the 100-meter freestyle race. He won a second gold medal as a member of the 4 x 200-meter relay team. Duke was proud of his participation in the first Olympics in which athletes took an oath to compete "for the glory of sport."

After Antwerp, the U.S. Olympic team toured Europe and the United States. Duke was mobbed wherever he went. He was so popular that a chaperone was appointed to protect him from adoring fans.

In 1922 Duke moved to California. He appeared in several Hollywood movies, usually playing "native chiefs" because he was dark skinned. Duke always performed with dignity but wished directors would sometimes cast him in roles that were not such stereotypes.

When not acting Duke took part in swimming exhibitions and gave surfing demonstrations across the country. He experimented with surfboard design and worked on making hollow boards. He also made himself a small, light board that he took everywhere.

Duke held the record as the fastest swimmer in the world for twelve years. When the 1924 Olympic Games in Paris, France, came up, he was determined to remain the champion despite strong competition from the young American swimmer Johnny Weissmuller. Using the flutter kick Duke had made famous, Weissmuller broke Duke's existing Olympic record with a speed of 59 seconds in the 100-meter freestyle. Duke accepted the second-place silver medal with a gracious smile.

Duke kept training, swimming, and surfing. He thought he had a good chance of beating Weissmuller in the 1928 Olympic Games in Amsterdam, Netherlands, but Duke was sidelined by illness. By the end of his Olympic career in 1932 at age forty-one, Duke had won three gold medals, two silver medals, and one bronze.

To Duke surfing was a way of life, and one day in 1925 in Southern California he proved that surfboards could also save lives.

Big surf was expected at Corona del Mar, and Duke and two friends had spent the night sleeping on the beach. While checking out the huge, green waves in the foggy morning, Duke noticed a fishing boat making its way close to the coast. Suddenly a great wave curled forward and capsized the boat.

Grabbing his board, Duke sprang into action. He paddled out into the raging ocean and dragged four drowning fishermen onto his surfboard. He commanded the panicked men to lock their arms around the board. The surfboard somersaulted and then bounced into the shallows. With the men safe, Duke ran back into the water, searching out the feeble calls for help, pulling fishermen onto his board and taking them in to shore. His friends also entered the wild sea on their boards, searching for survivors.

Duke saved eight people that day and his friends rescued four. Saddened that they had not saved everyone, Duke hurried from the beach before he could be thanked and before news reporters arrived. Later the actions of Duke and his friends were described as "the most superhuman rescue act and finest display of surf-riding ever seen in the world." Duke was pleased when surfboards became standard equipment on emergency rescue trucks and at lifeguard towers.

Duke moved back to his island home in 1930. He had done so much to promote Hawai'i and surfing around the world, people insisted there should be a place of honor for him at home. Friends encouraged Duke to run for public office as sheriff of Honolulu. In 1934 he won easily, and he remained Honolulu's sheriff for twenty-six years.

In 1940, when he was fifty, Duke married Nadine Alexander. Twenty years earlier, as a teenager in Boston, she had fallen in love with his picture. When an opportunity to teach dancing in Hawai'i came along in 1938, Nadine jumped at the chance. One of Duke's brothers eventually introduced them, and it was love at first sight.

Hawai'i became the fiftieth state of the United States in 1959, and the sheriff's position was abolished. Duke then became the official state of Hawai'i Ambassador of Aloha. He welcomed politicians, celebrities, and other distinguished guests and officiated at countless events and celebrations.

Duke thought of surfing as Hawai'i's gift to the world, and he never stopped promoting the sport. In his lifetime Duke saw surfing grow into a multibillion-dollar pastime enjoyed by millions. He loved watching young surfers discover the thrill of riding the waves.

Duke's dream, yet to be fulfilled, was that one day surfing would be an event in the Olympic Games and that surfers would compete for Olympic gold in the thundering ocean waves.

Duke Paoa Kahanamoku, "the Father of Modern Surfing," died on January 22, 1968, at the age of seventy-seven. He was the world's greatest waterman and the twentieth century's most influential surfer. Just as important, Duke will always be remembered for his kindness and modesty, good sportsmanship, and love of life. "No matter what he did, he spread aloha."

DUKE'S CREED OF ALOHA

In Hawai'i we greet friends, loved ones or strangers
with Aloha, which means with love.
Aloha is the key word to the universal spirit of real
hospitality, which makes Hawai'i renowned as the
world's center of understanding and fellowship.
Try meeting or leaving people with Aloha.
You'll be surprised by their reaction.
I believe it and this is my creed.
Aloha to you.

HIGHLIGHTS OF DUKE KAHANAMOKU'S LIFE AND LEGACY

1890 August 24: Born in Honolulu, Hawai'i

1900 Organic Act makes citizens of Republic of Hawai'i citizens of the United States

1910 Hawaiian Amateur Athletic Union created

1911 Organized Hui Nalu, Club of the Waves

August 12: First Amateur Athletic Union-Hawai'i sanctioned swim meet held in Honolulu Harbor; broke world records in 50-yard, 100-yard, and 220-yard freestyle races

1912 Olympic Games in Stockholm, Sweden; won gold medal in 100-meter freestyle race and silver medal in 4 x 200-meter freestyle relay

Introduced surfing to United States east coast

1914–1915 Introduced surfing to Australia and New Zealand

1915–1932 Helped popularize surfing and swimming in California

1916 Olympic Games in Berlin, Germany, canceled

1917 Rode monster wave in Waikīkī for one and three-quarter miles

1918 Swam in exhibitions to raise money for Liberty Loan War Bonds to support United States efforts in World War I

1920 Olympic Games in Antwerp, Belgium; won gold medals in 100-meter freestyle race and 4 x 200-meter freestyle relay

1922–1930 Lived in Los Angeles, California; played small roles in movies

1924 Olympic Games in Paris, France; won silver medal in 100-meter freestyle race

1925 Rescued eight people on surfboard at Corona del Mar, California

1932 Olympic Games in Los Angeles, California; won bronze medal as alternate member of water polo team

1934–1960 Served as Sheriff of City and County of Honolulu

1940 August 2: Married Nadine Alexander

1956 Attended Olympic Games in Melbourne, Australia, as official U.S. representative; recommended surfing as an Olympic event

1959 Hawai'i became fiftieth state of the United States

1960 Appointed official state of Hawai'i Ambassador of Aloha

1964 Honored as Sports Champion of the Century at New York World's Fair

1965 December: First Duke Kahanamoku Invitational Surfing Championships held at Sunset Beach, O'ahu, Hawai'i

1965–1966 One of first group inducted into International Swimming Hall of Fame and Surfing Hall of Fame

1968 January 22: Died in Honolulu

January 27: Thousands attended Waikīkī Beach funeral

1969 Plaque and bust dedicated at Huntington Beach, California

1984 Inducted into U.S. Olympic Hall of Fame

1986 Outrigger Duke Kahanamoku Foundation created

1990 Statue dedicated at Waikīkī Beach, Hawai'i

1994 Statue dedicated at Freshwater Beach, Sydney, Australia

First name inscribed in Huntington Beach Surfing Walk of Fame

1999 Named Surfer of the Century by *Surfer* magazine

2002 August 24: Duke Kahanamoku commemorative stamp issued by United States Postal Service